Omo

Endogo book 3

Published by Crossbridge Books
Worcester
© Crossbridge Books 2025

ISBN 978-1-916945-12-8

British Library Cataloguing Publication Data. A catalogue record for this book is available from the British Library.

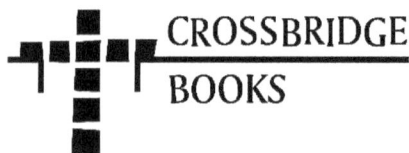

CROSSBRIDGE
BOOKS

Omo

Endogo book 3

by R M Price-Mohr

Vocabulary for book 3:

all
away
back
but
can
friendly
have
mother
not
Omo
on
ride
run
see
seen
tenrec
their
too
wet
will

Foreword for teachers

These books have been developed for older beginner readers. The research-based approach focuses on the recognition of just 100 key words that together make up approximately two-thirds of all reading matter in English.

For each new book, twenty new words are introduced and listed at the beginning of each book The new vocabulary for each book should be introduced to the learner in such a way that they will be able to recognise them at sight <u>before</u> reading the book. It is recommended that this is achieved through playing with the printed words. In the first instance, this should be by having two sets of printed and separated words in large font (minimum 20 point) that the beginner reader can match. It is crucial that the teacher continuously verbalise the words, and they may point to significant features in words, firstly the initial letters and secondly to any other distinctive features, to assist with the matching. Following this, the word recognition can be reinforced in games such as bingo, dominoes, snap, Pelmanism etc.

It is crucial that the teacher continue to verbalise the words during all the games, and the teacher should draw attention to the first letter of words and sound out that initial letter for the beginner.

Some temptations to avoid:

- Do not ask the reader to sound out all the individual letters of a word – only the initial letter has value at this stage for reading.
- Do not test the reader to see if they can recognise any of the words by telling you what they say – this should become obvious during the games; remember that visual recognition is not the same thing as verbalising what is seen.

The wet green rain forest.

This is Omo the endogo.

This is a friendly tenrec.

Omo can ride on the back of the tenrec.

This tenrec is friendly but his mother is not.

Max has seen the mother tenrec.

Kat can see the mother tenrec too.

Omo can see Max and Kat.

They have all seen the mother tenrec.

They will have to run away.

They all run back home to their cave.

High Frequency Words:

all
away
back
but
can
have
mother
on
run
seen
will

Word patterns:

_ee_   see
        seen
        green